All Things Touched
By Wind

For Dave,

who loves the

Klamath Basin too —

John Daniel

November 95

All Things Touched By Wind

John Daniel

SALMON RUN PRESS

Anchorage   *   San Francisco

Copyright © 1994 by John Daniel
Cover photograph copyright © 1994 by Robert Marsten

ISBN 0-9634000-5-3

All rights reserved
Printed in the United States of America
First Edition

All inquiries and permissions requests should
be addressed to the publisher.

99 98 97 96 95 94   5 4 3 2 1

Salmon Run Press
P. O. Box 231081
Anchorage, AK 99523-1081

Fifty copies have been bound
in cloth by Confluence Press,
Lewis-Clark State College,
Lewiston, Idaho.

For Marilyn

"In the mystery of what the world intends,
 How good the journey, hand in hand with you."

CONTENTS

Acknowledgements ix

Prologue: The Meal 3

I. *Outside Our Lives*

In Sky Lakes Wilderness 7
To Mt. St. Helens 8
To My Mother 9
The Pelicans of San Felipe 10
To William Stafford 11
The Canyon Wren 12
The Returns from Southern Utah: November 8, 1988 14
Nocturnal 15
Opal Creek 16
A Modern Man Speaks of Animals 18
Monument 20
To the Hidden Ones 21
Passage 22

II. *Here*

Here 25
The Echoing Lake 26
The Kid Who Asked Too Many Questions 27
For Our Fifth Anniversary, Seven Days Late 28
In Thanks for Feeling Happier 29
Iris 30
To the Scrub Jay on my Office Mate's Desk 32
The Gray Whales Passing Point Reyes 34

First Things First   36
The European Birch   37
A Suggestion to Myself for Dark Times   38
Dependence Day   39
Moment   40
A Prayer Among Friends   41
In Praise   42

III. *The Unseen*

The Unseen   45

Epilogue: *The Word*

Notes   60

ACKNOWLEDGEMENTS

These poems, some of them in different form, first appeared in the following magazines:

Calapooya Collage: "The Canyon Wren," "Iris," "To the Hidden Ones," "To William Stafford"

Earth First!: "The Returns from Southern Utah: November 8, 1988"

Fireweed: "The Unseen"

Kentucky Poetry Review: "First Things First"

Orion: "Monument"

Petroglyph: "Passage," "The Kid Who Asked Too Many Questions"

Poetry: "The Meal," "To The Scrub Jay on my Office Mate's Desk," "For Our Fifth Anniversary, Seven Days Late," part 12 of "The Unseen" (published as "The Rising Wind"), "The Echoing Lake," "In Sky Lakes Wilderness," "Dependence Day," "To My Mother"

The Seattle Review: "To Mt. St. Helens"

Sequoia: "The Gray Whales Passing Point Reyes"

Sierra: "A Suggestion to Myself for Dark Times"

The Southern Review: "Here," "In Thanks for Feeling Happier," "Opal Creek," "The Pelicans of San Felipe"

Zone 3: "The European Birch," "A Modern Man Speaks Of Animals," "Nocturnal," "A Prayer Among Friends," "In Praise," "The Word," "Moment"

Part 1 of "The Unseen" appeared in different form in *Common Ground* by John Daniel (Confluence Press, 1988) under the title "At Thirty-five." Reprinted by permission of Confluence Press.

"To William Stafford" also appeared in *Stafford's Road* (Adrienne Lee Press, 1991).

"Dependence Day" also appeared in *From Here We Speak*, Volume 4 of the Oregon Literature Series (Oregon State University Press, 1994).

For help of various kinds I'm grateful to Wendell Berry, Marilyn Daniel, W. S. Di Piero, John Ellison, Ken Fields, Jeff Harrison, John Laursen, Denise Levertov, Tom Sexton, and the members of the Portland poetry group, especially Jeff Berger, Jane Glazer, Bob McFarlane, John Morrison, Paulann Petersen, and Susan Spady. I thank John Smelcer, publisher of Salmon Run Press, for bringing this collection into print.

Prologue

The Meal

THE MEAL

The meat is before us, the flagons
have been filled, but my father
doesn't rise to speak. His head
is turned toward the spectacled man
who stares at his plate, and I've seen
that sharp white jaw in a picture —
my grandfather, the lawyer, the one
who died young of syphilis. The candles
glimmer his lenses, he doesn't look up.
Down the table in the crowd of faces
another comes clear, my father's
grandfather, the graybeard harnessmaker
they called *Grosspapa*, and more
beyond him that I almost know,
their faces obscuring, faint moons
in the dim smoky light. No one
has reached for a fork, the quiet
is awkward now, and I worry
for my father as I used to worry
when the whiskey drugged his tongue.
But he sits straight in his chair,
hands on the edge of the table,
his tie knotted tight. I feel
the familiar weight of his gaze
and a long time passes before
I can look, before I finally see
that the hurt his gray eyes held is gone,
they are clear and burning now,
and helplessly empty of words.
I understand that until I speak
the meal can't begin, all down
the long table they are staring
and waiting, they are hungry, the food
is before them, they have traveled
a great distance to be here.

I

Outside Our Lives

IN SKY LAKES WILDERNESS

Winter tells the old stories,
the lakes are shut like eyelids.
Earning heat to pay the wind
we thread our skis between dark firs,
pitch camp as the gray light leaves.
Our fire throws wild shadows
against the circling forest wall,
while beyond that little room
where we drink whiskey, laughing,
the cold stars glint, the wind
touches every tree. Later,
inside our tent, we feel the air
go still, a heaviness, and soon
the ticking of fine snowfall.
As we drift in and out of sleep
we hear the silent storm
begin to bury us, to mound us under
like the bowed young firs.
Our fire hisses faintly as snow
cools and covers it — nothing then
except the creak of limbs
taking on the slow, familiar weight,
and the small whistling flurries
of the wind. Anything we are
makes no difference in this place,
where trees, wind, and falling snow
work their ways together
in the stillness they have always known —
what strange joy, to huddle here
buried in our single warmth,
listening to what lives outside our lives.

TO MT. ST. HELENS

You were the perfect one,
the saint of symmetry.
We glanced at your benign
bright face, and you shined back
your blessing, you smiled
peacefully upon us.
We didn't much believe
your smoke and stir, we thought
your restiveness would pass —
and then you shuddered hard
and blasted yourself across
four states, engulfed a lake,
gorged rivers with gray mud,
flattened entire forests
and whatever lives they held
in your searing smother.
Your evenness and grace
exploded twelve miles high,
then showered down as grit
on our trim lawns and gardens —
and there you slouch, smudged
and gaping, spewing smoke,
resting in your rubble.
You did it, Mt. St. Helens.
As all of us looked on
you stormed in solitude,
you shrugged and shook aside
what we called beautiful
as if none of us were here,
no animals, no trees,
no life at all outside
your ancient fiery joy —
I admired you, mountain,
but I never loved you until now.

TO MY MOTHER

"I may not live much longer, you know,
and it's all right. I'm thankful
for everything I've had. Do you understand?"

I think I do. I know your eyes shine more
like the sky these days, a stillness
weights your shoulders, I know your swollen feet

and the bones that click in your wrist
when I take your hand can't bear you far.
Soon you are bound from this last house

to the world you love, the world
I love, and I will lose you there,
I will never touch your hand again.

But when tall pines stir with a rising wind,
when the river whispers past my camp,
when breakers sound beyond the brink of dunes,

I will know you by such signs
as I must have known you before I was,
when the anthem of your blood played round

and bathed me in power I breathed and breathed
until at last you could not hold me,
until at last you opened and gave me the world.

THE PELICANS OF SAN FELIPE

do most of their fishing asleep on the sand,
great bills lowered to their breasts.
Overhead the gulls scream *now*, and *now*,
but the pelicans drowse in the plenty of time —
the sand is warm, the breeze enfolds them,
the steady waves rumble and slosh.
Two or three together through the afternoon
they raise their monkish white heads
and lift from the sand, mute as in sleep,
winging their way above the green swells
to join the others now circling low,
and circling low, and each in its moment
with a tilt of the wings drops like a stone,
plummets without grace to smack the sea —
then bobbing up quickly, riding the swells,
wild gulls veering and screaming around them,
the pelicans lift their bills and swallow.

TO WILLIAM STAFFORD

Some would call it luck, I guess.
Stop to watch geese on the misty marsh
and something rises just beyond —
flash of head and tail, the great wings
shouldering slowly away. You said it
faithfully, with all your voices,
as you built the house of everything
your alertness could call forth —
geese on the marsh, the eagle rising,
it's a luck we can rely on
if we give ourselves to what's here.
Be ready, you said. *Out of the mist
of all indifferences, the world speaks.*
And that house of yours, the one
you worked on all those mornings,
the house of little things
we might have missed, the house
that stands by your allegiances
and walls nothing out — we're lucky
that you placed it here around us,
this home where you've welcomed us to live.

THE CANYON WREN

for Bruce Bowerman

All afternoon as we hiked up the canyon
with our echoing talk, we heard that bright
long-winded whistle stepping down the scale.
We never saw the bird — only a shadow,
a twitch of limb, as slight and quickly gone

as the lizards flicking across hot stones.
Where the streambed steepened to dry waterfall
we almost quit, our packs absurdly heavy,
the rocks we jarred loose clattering below,
that sky-filled notch of canyon drawing us on.

We camped by a few scummed pools, loud with frogs,
and climbing on in the morning we didn't find
the big surprise we'd talked of: no bighorn sheep,
no petroglyphs, no monster waterfall,
just more and more of tumbled boulders, clumps

of prickly pear, dry sand with fool's gold glint,
the same heat-shimmer in the same still air,
and once in a while, from somewhere close, the wren's
clear song. And then, that evening, something more.
We walked into the canyon's trick of quiet,

into the ease of being just where we were,
the great walls shouldering high, flooded with moon,
and down the gorge, Death Valley in pale haze.
As we sat late by crumbling coals, the wind
came glancing, grazing our faces, alive

in the limbs of the junipers, dying down now
and rising, returning its song. Across
cool stones, along the canyon's shadowed curves,
through all the secret slickrock passages
the wind came softly, and its voice spoke for our own.

THE RETURNS FROM SOUTHERN UTAH: NOVEMBER 8, 1988

On the Escalante this morning
sandstone voted to hold firm,
but the river was talking

big change. Grasses plotted
to win by numbers, deer
were listening to every side,

and under all cliffs the scree
was united — downhill, but slow.
Cottonwoods carried a motion

of wind, which quietly threw
its support to the hawks,
and with the sky wide open

to any suggestion, the sun
took a while to make up its mind
before it said *yes* to everything.

NOCTURNAL

Walking to my camp through trees
I swing my flashlight up
and a screech owl's yellow eyes
face mine. They bob and tilt,
shift sideways on the limb
as if trying to see me better —
enormous lamps, scruffed
with feathers and bits of claw
to fly them through the dark.
They stare, fixed and clear.
What am I to those eyes?
They flit to a higher limb.
With a quick flutter, they're gone.

I turn off the light and night
presses in, a blinding shimmer.
Black shapes loom. A stirring,
and again. The owl's call
comes softly, wavering quiet.
Not far through these trees
I've pitched a tent, but this
is no place that I know.

OPAL CREEK

A narrow, twisting trail enters this woods
of hemlock, red cedar, and Douglas fir,
follows the stream flashing white through trees,
switchbacks across steep ridges, and grows fainter
as the tilted, mossy-barked trees grow huger
and fallen trunks lie everywhere, roots upthrust,
their solid centuries drawn back to ground,
ranks of seedlings rooted in the rotting wood.

Grow and go down, the dark earth spiring to light
and returning, the forest travels its changing way
without the need of any trail to guide it,
and neither do the varied thrush and winter wren
need direction through the shadows where they sing,
or the red-backed vole that burrows in the ground,
or the stream spuming and swirling between pools.
Only we humans who walk here need this line

that leads through stillness and the muted light,
through ferns and thimbleberry sopping our pants,
through the blended dark smells of mossy ground,
through scatters of mushrooms yellow and crimson,
flaring orange, and others half-black half-white —
and even we can change, even women and men
can gradually learn to let go of the trail
as it fades among trees and underbrush

and leaves us where nothing human shows the way.
There are other ways. We can lower ourselves
on vine maple holds down a moss-slick bank,
thrash through a tangle of devil's club and briars,
climb from the thicket on a down Douglas fir
and walk that trunk to another, and another,
and at last to one great fallen tree, thicker through
than we are tall. We can climb its furrowed bark

and sit for a while, our hard breath easing
as we listen to a bird hidden high above.
Like the spiring trees and the lives they hold,
we rest ourselves on death's generous body,
and all around us where the stillness sings
we see the green abundance of death's rising.
We came for this, to join for an afternoon
the long dance of the trees, and when we go

to find the trail and walk out of the forest,
we take with us what surrounds us in this place
by leaving it here, where it belongs—
where mushrooms, moss, and red-backed vole,
where thimbleberry and dripping ferns,
where thrush and wren and the unseen birds,
where swirling stream and muted light,
where stillness and the ancient trees go on.

A MODERN MAN SPEAKS OF ANIMALS

Some who claim to speak for nature are saying
that even our names for animals are wrong.
Each species has a secret name, they say.
Deer identify themselves by twitching tails,
songbirds sing, the crickets chirp, etc.
And that's not all — those secret names, we're told,
are like some poem in a language we've forgotten,
and because we do not speak the tongue
we treat animals unfairly, we are cruel,
and we ourselves are diminished in some way.
Complete nonsense, of course. But for argument
let's say it's true — let's say that animals
are like a poem. There's no doubt that the poem
is beautiful, and no doubt that it's varied
and plentiful — so varied and plentiful,
most reasonable people would agree,
that even if we understood the language
no one could possibly know all the names.
And that being so, it follows clearly then
that we can't possibly be asked to know
each time a name no longer says itself.
When it's brought to our attention, we of course
regret the loss. No one can be happy
when a species disappears. But science shows
that others have gone silent all through time,
from meteors and ice and drought. Nature
has always worked that way — if there is cruelty
in the world, it comes from natural law itself,
not our human doings. But fortunately,
as we all know, nature abhors a vacuum.
Though certain names go quiet, the poem itself
flows on and on. Where those names were

a million more now sound themselves, a comfort
and a pleasure around our busy days —
sparrows flock to the window feeder,
deer bound gracefully across the road,
giraffes and lions delight us in our zoos.
And even if it's true what some are claiming,
that because we live as we choose to live
the vanishing of names comes faster now —
every day, they would have us believe —
there is no proof, but even if it's true,
perspective is important. The poem is lovely,
we all know that, but we also know by now —
to speak quite frankly — it sings of a world
we've left behind, it sings in a foreign tongue
we have no need for now. It's our own words
that must properly concern us, the names
we understand and speak together —
economy, technology, humanism, progress —
and our business is to keep on saying them,
to know them well and say them clearly, say them loud,
there is no reason that we can't speak them endlessly,
regardless of what happens outside our lives.

MONUMENT

If it was wood they came for, wood was here.
But every tree? Stumps and scraped earth now,
heaps of mud-smeared boughs and splintered sticks.
The smell of sap hangs everywhere. Ferns
and sorrel patch the hillside, bright with rain.
Chickadees hop and rasp, a crow flies by,
but whatever else lived here is dead or gone.
The very genius of these hills, the soil
that gathered rain and changing light for centuries,
that gave forth green and towering stillnesses
as it slowly deepened here — it's leaving too.
It's washing down in gullies to a muddy stream.

TO THE HIDDEN ONES

You of our own bodies magnified,
who glide through forest with the quiet of trees,
stay away from us — we are hungry.
If you stray too close
we will tear you into facts,
we will eat you as we eat everything
we don't understand, you will swell
the certainty that bloats us and leaves us starving.

Save yourselves, save us from our dull knowledge.
Show us only your riverbank track,
a brief shadow
where you vanish among trees.
As you pass in the mountain night
let one twig snap,
and falling quiet in the gaze of your unseen eyes
we will shiver, we will hear
the wind in its distances,
the stars above us will burn bright.

PASSAGE

To listen to the river's muted voice,
its licks and gurgles
along the bank,
is to hear the soundlessness of snow
come down in all its multitudes
on heights of rock,
to hear that stillness
sink gradually down,
grow old and heavy,
dense with time,
dense with cold,
then quicken at last
beneath slow glacial tongues,
milky streamings
over stone,
trickling now,
splashing down, gathering
in gravity's song,
boulder music pounding on
with sprays of spume
and swirling pools,
and settling through distances
to slide past here,
subdued and lively, filled
with a dreamer's speechful stirring,
lost in its old story that never ends.

II

Here

HERE

If you'll close your eyes and light the inner dark
you'll see a field, a grassy plain extending
to a line of far blue hills, and as you walk
you'll feel the brushing softness of the grass,
its coolness underfoot. You have no memory
of where or why you started, you only know
that the speck you've been approaching rises whole
before you now, a solitary tree
of long and curving limbs, its deep green leaves
shimmering with the breeze that laves your face,
and through the play of leaves you see
the blue of sky, a few bright clouds, the range
of distant hills. Improbable that a tree
stands here, and you stand too, the steady ground
beneath you, and all around the lively air —
but unlikely as it is, this is the place
where you've arrived, the place you've never seen
yet recognize, the rendezvous no one arranged.
You can't stay long, you're traveling to the hills
and won't return, so look carefully once more
before you leave. Hills, field, the shimmering tree—
how is it that you're here, to stand and see?

THE ECHOING LAKE

for John Stacey

Cadence of our hissing skis, soft crunch of poles,
across the lake's clear calm we push and glide,
the fresh snow glittering with sparks of moon,
and circling round as if for ceremony,
the black upthrusted points of silent trees.

We slogged in miles for this, to solve our lives
for just an evening by this algebra
of light and dark, and the world will never stand
in stricter clarity — yet how we fit
in its cold beauty isn't clear. The moon's

blank face says nothing, and around it flares
a text of glinting hieroglyphic fire
our minds can't comprehend, inscrutable
as our own shadows skiing next to us,
as the sharply spiring silhouettes of trees.

But listen — when we stop and sing the tones
just right, those dark hemlocks and Douglas firs
enclose us in the chord of our own voices,
hovering like our breath-clouds in the cold,
shimmering with the flashing snow and stars.

THE KID WHO ASKED
TOO MANY QUESTIONS

All our walk long the boy had wondered
why some rocks were big and some
not so big, why this tree died
and that one lived, why juniper berries
were the blue of sky — so bye and bye
I grumbled up a thunderstorm
and lightning split him eye for eye.
His halves settled, two gray stones
stuck in the ground with no voice
to ask, "What happened?" Between them,
where all that wanting to know
had seethed behind the boy's eyes,
the yellow balsamroot blooms in May,
and lizards wait for a question
to the answer beneath their feet.

FOR OUR FIFTH ANNIVERSARY, SEVEN DAYS LATE

Milestones mark only a length of road,
not those who walk it, and our birthdays prove
only that calendars keep good time.

We count us differently. The numbered years
count less than what they slowly pearl around us,
around our pleasures and our irritations,

the gradual surprise of this shared life,
this mingling that we wear. We count on that,
and though I know that no arithmetic

can make us more than we are, I also know
five years and seven days are not our sum,
and whatever else I am, I know I'm here —

a happy man tapping my foot to music,
counting the time (in my forgetful way)
to this singular song we learn day by day.

IN THANKS FOR FEELING HAPPIER

The wind that wakes the aspen leaves
rises from its absence into song —
spirit remembers, stirs itself,
sings now without intent to sing,
aimlessly and exactly sure,
a shimmering in sunlit air.

IRIS

in memory of Tom Carlos

Three tight-wrapped buds that hadn't changed in days
have burst overnight
into yellow blooms, fresh
with light and lemony scent
this morning that my friend is dead — he
who lived with his pack by the door,
who hammered silver into rings and bracelets
and drove the show circuit
stoked on coffee across the West,
selling and trading
from his little crammed car,
talking and talking,
who taught camp kids
that thronged him like puppies
how to pinch and coil,
how to pick dry cow dung
to fire their pots
and laugh off the ones that shattered,
who grinned around his drooping mustache
sweaty-faced by the fire
with a bottle of bad wine
telling the same stories he told last year
and laughing, laughing,
bellowing to the pines and starry sky
from his t-shirted chest
where his heart danced on
in the flow of his days
then gave him an hour or two to be scared
and stopped —

yanked him from life at 42
as fast as these blooms
burst open from buds
to flash here, finished, in the late morning sun.

TO THE SCRUB JAY ON MY
OFFICE MATE'S DESK

As if you know what you're doing
you flick through the window
and here you are, brighter blue
than I've ever seen you in sun,
at ease and cocking your head
as if born for the company
of Kent's papers and cups.
I'll be late for class, stout-bill,
but I have to know why you flew in
to this fluorescent cave
from the air of a fine spring day,
and what's on your mind
as you hop past the stapler —

and how I can keep you
from the half-open door
just a wing-lift away.
Don't do it, bird.
I can just see you
lost in the halls, slapping
the ceiling tiles, glancing
off dim-painted walls,
careening into my class
with your croaking panic
and dodging the startled faces,
flapping and clawing, grazing
the blackboard, finally thrashing
your chalk-smeared feathers
against the window, crazy
for the blue afternoon. *That*
might arouse their interest.

But you have better sense.
With a flex of your legs,
a brush of air on my cheek,
you leave as you came. You're out
where you should be. I'm left
with the half-open door.

THE GRAY WHALES PASSING POINT REYES

With geysering spouts the whales break into sun and plunge
    steady southward, flukes tossed high
and sliding under sea. All afternoon they pass, three and four
    at a time, still weeks away

from the Baja lagoons where they'll roll belly to belly
    and birth their young,
six thousand miles from the Arctic ice to lounge a month
    in those warm seas —

those seas where Scammon's men a century ago speared calves
    to get the mothers, spouts
shooting blood, flukes thrashing the water to crimson froth,
    and the salt flats stinking of peeled bones

as the northern prairies stank of bison shot from trains,
    stripped of tongue and three-dollar hide . . .
that square-shouldered pleasure bringing big things down.
    We aim binoculars now, shoot

only pictures, crowding the lighthouse rail and exclaiming
    as a new spout rises,
a glistening back breaks water and plunges away.
    Steadily, easily

they move with the urge that drives them, huge bodies small
    in the spangled sea
and small in the scope of their great journey, traveling
    this trail of rough-rocked coast

that in March they'll follow north again, the new calves
    swimming alongside their mothers
to the Bering Sea's blue cold. We watch and keep watching
    as if hypnotized, not by the creatures

we see only for seconds but by the long unfaltering line
    of their passage, continuing on
through the afternoon and steadily on in the hazy dusk
    as we drift from the rail

and blend in the highway's flow — bright stream that bears us
    to the dinners and sleeps
of our singular lives, and each of us on to new places,
    new homes, travels and travels

but no journey together like the journey of the whales,
    no path that might gather us
and lead us around through the turning of seasons and back
    to ourselves, again and again,

looping our one life through the lengths of Earth's time.

FIRST THINGS FIRST

Dreaming, when I ask Wendell Berry
for seeds, his hands turn the leaves
of a bulky loose book, bulging
with woven and waxpaper pouches —
specks, fat kernels, wings and barbs,
corn and ricegrass tucked under straps,
tufts of wheat and long-eared oats
on the pages his hands keep turning.
"What kind did you want?" he says.
I forgot as the pages went by.
"Where do you live?" he's asking now,
and I know, of course, or thought I did . . .
"Well, take what you want," he says,
and grins. "But don't you think
you'll need a place to plant 'em?"

THE EUROPEAN BIRCH

for Denise Levertov

The white trunk's wet gleaming,
scarred, flecked with moss,
the fountaining
of leafless limbs and twigs — where
but in this rain
does the birch belong?
Half the world
from the birthplace of its kind,
it gathers
the falling formlessness
so that each twig-tip
and joint of twig
bears one clear drop,
one cosmos
glowing from within,
each held in wholeness
by the sheer
tension of its forming,
and the drops all together
this autumn afternoon
show the birch
in its distinction, standing clear.

A SUGGESTION TO MYSELF FOR DARK TIMES

Late in the night when no direction I walk
leads out of sadness, when my own life
feels lost to me, and everything I've done
seems wrong or not enough, what can I lose
if I abandon the lights I've been living by
and travel to a place where the land lies flat
and clear, where the luminous Milky Way
spreads specked and glittering across the sky.
The faint abundance of that distant fire
falls all around me — so that's where I'll walk,
I'll walk a long time out among those stars
until I'm not so sure in their wild light
just where I am or where I started,
until the shimmering cosmos burns so bright
it seems I am that fire and always was,
adrift through time's dark distances.
And the fire seethed once in a whirling cloud
and the cloud was me, it was me
that spewed and surged in molten torrents
and cooled, heavy, as the great rains fell.
It was me holding still when all that moved
was wind on water, and me that stirred,
a speck in the deeps where hot vents flowed —
and the speck splitting away was also me,
and all those slippery surfaces as I changed
again and again, churning tail, fins and gills,
the mouth that first sucked air was mine,
mine were the feet that found their way,
that carried my shifting and shifting self,
the carefully listening ears were mine,
the eyes gazing across the land, and up
at the far-strewn brilliance of night —
my own forgotten face shines there,
and where in this bright heaven could I be lost?

DEPENDENCE DAY

It would be a quieter holiday, no fireworks
or loud parades, no speeches, no salutes to any flag,
a day of staying home instead of crowding away,
a day we celebrate nothing gained in war
but what we're given—how the sun's warmth
is democratic, touching everyone,
and the rain is democratic too,
how the strongest branches in the wind
give themselves as they resist, resist
and give themselves, how birds could have no freedom
without the planet's weight to wing against,
how Earth itself could come to be
only when a whirling cloud of dust
pledged allegiance as a world
circling dependently around a star, and the star
blossomed into fire from the ash of other stars,
and once, at the dark zero of our time,
a blaze of revolutionary light
exploded out of nowhere, out of nothing,
because nothing needed the light,
as the brilliance of the light itself needs nothing.

MOMENT

for W. S. Di Piero

Squares of tended grass, roses
trimmed and mulched with chips, all
the blank front doors along
these gridded streets, neighborhood
I walk and carry docilely
in walks of mind — until
one yellow leaf shoots by
and I'm on edge again, I'm
walking fast through gusting air
that strips the maples, scattering
leaves and paper scraps
like some rousing consciousness
unbound by human blocks — as if
the wild god had wakened me,
or waked in me, not the clerk
who accounts for fallen birds,
the one we kicked upstairs,
but the god still ranging
in this world, that scatters us
to its unspoken need, and only
finds its way as we find ours.

A PRAYER AMONG FRIENDS

Among the other wonders of our lives, we're alive
with one another, we walk here in the light
of this unlikely world that isn't ours for long.
May we spend generously the time we are given.
May we enact our responsibilities as thoroughly
as we enjoy our pleasures. May we see with clarity,
may we seek a vision that serves all beings,
may we honor the mystery surpassing our sight.
And this above all — may we hold in our hands
the gift of good work and bear it forth whole,
as we were borne forth by a power we praise
to this one Earth, this homeland of all we love.

IN PRAISE

High in the pines the rising night wind lifts me awake
to stars and silhouettes of shifting trees,
their boughs alive with a passing spirit
whose deep sounding stirs in me
an older, vaster spirit
streaming from the source of time—
spirit that breathed these trees into being,
the ground that holds them as they sway,
and I who lie here listening,
told in a tongue I almost know
of where I came from and what I am,
how the power that imagined me moves through me
and beyond, far past my own imaginings
of what it is, and beautiful the flowing of its song.

III

The Unseen

THE UNSEEN

1

Mustard crowds the barbed-wire fence,
the entire hillside thick with light
and glowing brighter as the pale sky
goes dim. The single oak is hazed
with April leaves. Across the valley
children call, quick strokes of sound.
A wavering cloud of sparrows passes,
a kestrel hovers on beating wings—
impossibly much, but I need more tonight
than the bare glory of what's given.
I need to rub this moment in mind
for the shimmer of meaning I almost see,
I need the boy who stood shivering once
in a different field, hands clenched
at his sides in the clammy dusk
as he silently burned into mind
the whippoorwills, silhouettes of trees,
the bright clear blue of the west—
I'll remember, he whispered, *even
when I'm dead I'll remember this.*

2

It ends in emptiness, a dark wind,
the light of cold stars
passing through me —
once I breathed,
I walked in my body.
Nothing, I don't know,
I say when my mother asks
what made me cry,
and as the light goes out —
switch on, switch off — I know
that even the dream is wrong,
that when I die
there will be no stars,
nothing in my mind,
no *me*,
and I will not return in all of time.

3

Birdsong woke me to the hunger.
As pale light filled the window
I watched with one eye open,
wondering what I wanted —
nothing in my parents' house
or school or Sunday school
but something I had never tasted,
something in the still trees,
the songs of hidden birds
calling in the cool morning
as I still slept, it was nowhere
in the world or everywhere,
if I could just find words to name it.

4

I lay on the pavement trying to see.
The snake raised his broken neck,
swaying, as if
there was something he still needed.
I was looking for the moment.
His jaws stretched, and from deep
in the darkness of his throat
a dry hiss forced its way.
In a spasm, he subsided.
It was the spirit leaving him,
I told myself, pressing
at the skin of his small piled body.
He twitched and lay still.
I heard the spirit,
I said out loud, and stood
in the stillness of the summer afternoon.

5

I'd sit where the trunk divided
and watch how the limbs
divided again,
how they branched and branched
and made themselves
a confusion of a million twig-ends
touching air.
And I wondered —
if a bud on one twig-end
awakened
by itself in air,
if all it saw
was twigs and buds,
the empty sky,
could it ever know
where it came from?
Before it fell,
could it think its way back through
those chance divisions,
through all
the blind branching history
that brought it to its lonely place
from the one
where it was born?

6

Kneeling by the animal tracks I didn't know,
I felt hidden eyes
upon me, close, and everything
stood clearer, brighter then,
each twig, each fallen leaf
in the puddles from the morning's rain.
Hiking home through woods and fields
where nothing moved but me,
watched by something wild
that stirred my groin and made me whirl around
to stare at stones and honeysuckle,
at the hillside's green horizon,
the shining of last light on boughs —
those things meant more
than just themselves, they stood
for all the things I couldn't know
as I walked home,
hollow-bellied with happiness,
beneath the darkening forest trees
and the bright scattered tracks of all the stars.

7

Wind on the waters, rippling there,
rippling in the reeds
that gracefully give way
and rest. And now
downshore the rippling reeds,
now here again,
the water stirs and quickens —
if it were given I would come back, if
it were given
I would roam here always,
touching the face of what I loved.

8

Fired with sun, the red-tail drifts
deep in the sky, circling
higher and higher
in that field of light,
and drowsing below
I dream and drift along,
I feel the streaming air,
the land turning beneath me —
to die might feel like this,
my speck of self ascending
so far into the light
that it becomes the light at last.
And as I rise to go
I see in the grass
two yellow slugs,
curled close in semi-circles
stroking each other with their snouts,
stretching filaments of slime
as they stroke. They raise
their blind, faceless mouths,
they stir themselves in the light of sun.

9

This is the path where the panther waits,
shadowing the things of day.
His eyes glow. I call them stars.
His breath stirs. I call it wind.
His black coat quickens, and this
is the place I always falter,
this is the shadow
of his unborn leap,
where he waits to rend
my hide of fear,
where I might be born,
or disappear.

10

Paralyzed, I saw
my heart gone still.
I couldn't reach
to squeeze and pound it
back to life. Arteries
grew stiff around it.
I gave up then.
And from those roots
and the cold stone
they circumscribed,
a great tree grew —
I watched it rise,
watched it swaying
in the light of sky,
and I felt my body
stretch and tremble.

11

High to the north a snow peak stands in the last
deep light,
the nameless one
that sends this black-water stream
swirling through the chill of dusk.
Nothing
in the stream's quick passing,
nothing in the snow
and silent trees,
nothing in the mountain glowing with final sun
knows my presence,
and nothing will be lessened
when I've gone.
It isn't much,
this shivering warmth
I cradle like a candle,
worried how it flickers,
how it burns down —
I would let it burn,
I would turn it loose
to the beautiful indifference of this world,
where the first stars
are shining,
the mountain stands in stillness,
and the stream swirls
past one small light in the darkening trees.

12

If the way is anywhere, it's here
in the dodge and mingle of mustard flowers
flattening as the wind comes on,
in the blue eucalyptus swirling wild
with a shimmer of water-sound,
and even in the stiff oak limbs
that stir as if remembering just now
what motion is. It doesn't seem
so difficult, this fluid aimlessness,
this ease with which things bend
as they hold firm — what flows in trees
and ripples silvery through the grass
is loosening my fear-bound spirit
that thinking tried and tried to free.
If I can learn this limbering,
if I can dance this earthly dance
like all things touched by wind,
when the hour comes I might be ready
to swirl loose from all I know.

Epilogue

The Word

THE WORD

The last and truest of all these words
is the one that won't be said,
that almost forms upon my tongue
as I listen
for its missing shape of sound
in wind and running water,
in the stillness of the misted field.
I hold it like a stone
I have no name for, blankly smooth
to every touch —
I stare and watch it always change
into things I already know.
I strike it,
break it down to its brief syllables
and peer among them
for the secret it withholds,
and when that fails
as all else fails, I turn
to the fractured light of stars,
this brilliant wilderness
that somehow spells the word I love,
the word I lose
each time it starts to say itself,
the word
for which I make this home and pass it on.

Notes

To Mt. St. Helens

The school children of La Grande, Oregon, helped me see the mountain's joy, as did Ursula Le Guin in her essay "A Very Warm Mountain."

The Canyon Wren

The phrase "trick of quiet" I borrow from Sherwood Anderson by way of Wallace Stegner. Anderson wrote in a letter to Waldo Frank: "I can remember old fellows in my home town speaking feelingly of an evening spent on the big empty plains. It had taken the shrillness out of them. They had learned the trick of quiet . . ." Stegner quotes this passage in his "Wilderness Letter."

Opal Creek

The Opal Creek drainage, in the central Oregon Cascades, contains the largest remaining stands of unprotected old-growth forest in the state. Parts of the forest have long been scheduled for logging by the U. S. Forest Service. So far, friends of the place have been able to preserve it.

The Gray Whales Passing Point Reyes

Charles Scammon was one of the captains who hunted the California gray whale almost to extinction around the end of the nineteenth century. The species is now protected by law and beginning to thrive again.

Raised in the suburbs of Washington, D. C., John Daniel has lived in the West since 1966. He has worked as a college student, logger, railroad inspector, rock climbing instructor, hod carrier, and poet-in-the-schools. In 1982 he received a Wallace Stegner Fellowship in Poetry at Stanford University, where he then taught for five years as a lecturer in creative writing and composition. Daniel is poetry editor of *Wilderness* Magazine and the author of one previous book of poems, *Common Ground* (Confluence Press, 1988). *The Trail Home*, a collection of his essays on nature, imagination, and the American West, was published in 1992 by the West Coast office of Pantheon Books. Daniel and his wife Marilyn, a weaver and environmental engineer, live near Eugene, Oregon.